Ardzie Meets Sully The Bully

Story By Miss Veronica

Illustrations by Tony Mangum

Dymond Publishing
www.sullythebully.com

To order additional copies of this book, contact:
Dymond Publishing

Email: publishing@dymondbusinesses.com
Website: www:sullythebully.com

Together we can stop bullying.

Bullying is unwanted behavior that has been plaguing our society far too long. It exists because we allow it to exist. Bullying has caused many people to become ill, depressed, and even commit suicide. As a society, we must do whatever is necessary to eliminate this evil. Miss Veronica asserts that as concerned citizens, we must bombard our society with positive actions and words and must not tolerate any aspect of bullying. We must actively engage in activities to get rid of this unnecessary bad behavior.

Ardzie Meets Sully,The Bully is a story aimed at fighting bullying simply by using the "Just Be Nice" concept; that is, saying nice words and performing nice actions.

The author believes that if we all practice the "Just Be Nice" concept and make it a part of our everyday lives, we can eventually live in a society free of bullying.

Why not try it? What do we have to lose? BULLYING, that's what!

Hello. This is Ardzie and he's an aardvark. Let's see what happens when he meets Sully. Sully is an aardvark too, but he's a bully.

Aardvark

That's a funny word.

Do you know what an aardvark is?

Do you know what a bully is?

Do you know what a bully does?

Let's see what Ardzie and Sully do in the story.

Ardzie didn't want to go to his new school today.

He knew that the kids were going to tease him. The kids at his old school always teased him.

So, he thought that the kids at the new school would tease him too.

He had to wear big eyeglasses that made him look funny.

He talked funny too.

But, most of all, he had those awful green spots on his face and snout.

Oh, yes, he knew that today was going to be a BAD day.

What a way to start at his new school.

As Ardzie entered the school, a group of aardvarks were standing in the hallway.

One of them looked at Ardzie with a smirk on his face. "Hey polka dots! What's your name? Is it Polkie?"

Ardzie didn't say anything, just walked pass them as they started laughing.

Katie heard what Sully said. She walked over to the group, and with her hands on her hips, she said, "Sully, apologize right now!"

"How would you feel if someone called you names?"

"Do it now, Sully...apologize!" Katie demanded. Sully reluctantly apologized to Ardzie. "Sorry."

During class, Ms. Vark asked Ardzie to tell the class about himself.

Ardzie stuttered when he talked, so he had a really hard time sharing with the class. Sully snickered as soon as Ardzie started talking.

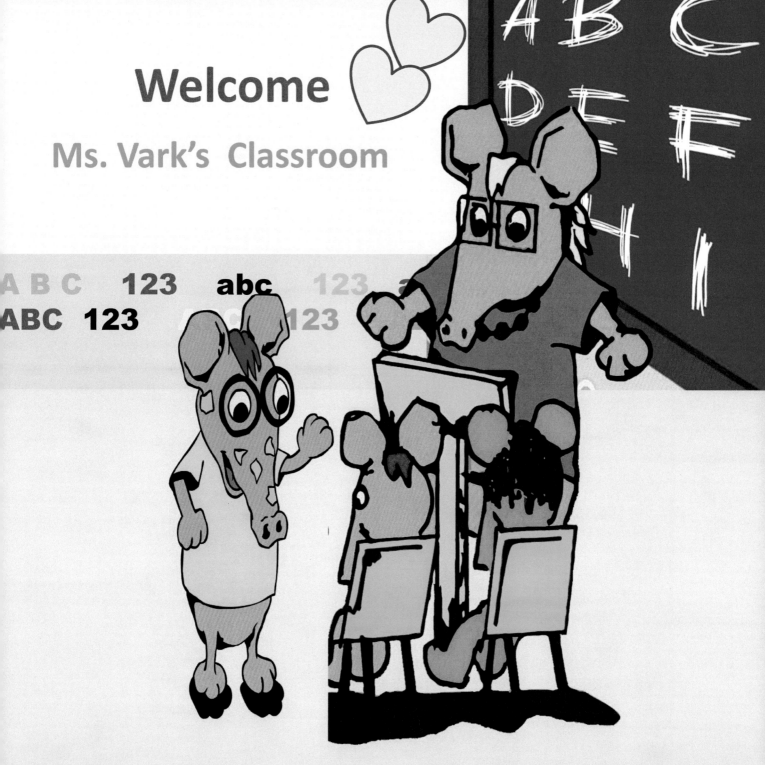

Ms. Vark told Sully it was not nice of him to snicker at Ardzie. She asked Sully if he would want someone snickering at him. Sully told her "No."

"Well, you should be nice then and not laugh at him,"

Ms. Vark said.

"But, Ms. Vark he talks funny and he does not look like us. See those polka dots on his face? He's just weird," said Sully.

"Well, Ardzie may say the same thing about you since you don't look like him. How would you feel if Ardzie teased you, or if he called you names?", Ms. Vark asked.

"I would feel bad," said Sully.

"Sure you would," said Ms. Vark. " It's better to be nice."   Sully agreed.

Later at the playground, Sully was all over the place.

He pulled Katie's hair.

He knocked Joey to the ground on purpose.

He jumped from behind a tree and made Sarah spill her juice.

He did not wait his turn at the water fountain, but jumped in front of Sandy.

Ms. Vark saw what Sully was doing and made him come sit beside her on the bench for the remainder of recess.

She talked to Sully about how he was acting and not being nice to his classmates. Ms. Vark told him that his classmates feel sad when he is not nice to them.

Sully didn't want his classmates to be sad, so he promised Ms. Vark that he would do better. He would just be nice.

As he watched the other aardvarks playing, Sully thought about his floppy ears. They didn't stand up straight like everyone else's.

No one teased him about them. They did not tease him about his hair that did not lay flat on his head.

Sully decided he was going to change his ways. He was not going to be a bully anymore.

At the end of recess, Sully promised Ms. Vark he was going to be nice.

Sully soon forgot the promise he made to Ms. Vark.

During coloring period, he didn't have a blue crayon that he needed to color the sky in his picture.

He went over to Ardzie's desk. Ardzie had all the color crayons, including a blue one.

Sully reached down and picked up the box of crayons. Without asking Ardzie, Sully took the blue crayon and started back to his desk.

All of a sudden he remembered his promise to Ms. Vark : "just be nice". He would not want anyone taking anything from him without asking.

He turned around and did the right thing. He asked Ardzie if he could borrow his blue crayon.

Ardzie told him yes and continued to color his picture. Sully went back to his desk and started coloring his picture too.

Sully felt good and so did Ardzie.

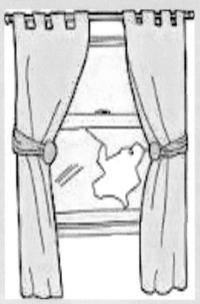

The next day, Ardzie decided to wear a new cap that his father had given him. It had a lot of colors on it, and Ardzie thought it was cool looking.

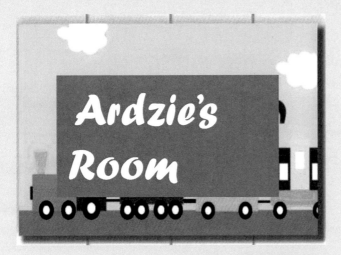

As soon as Ardzie walked into the school, there was Sully.

Sully came up to him smiling. "New hat?" he asked.

"Yep," answered Ardzie. He held his breath, not knowing what Sully was going to do or say next.

"Oh, it's cool. The colors look good on you," Sully said.

Thanks, Ardzie said, "I like your shirt. It's cool too."

After they finished admiring each other, Ardzie and Sully went into the classroom.

They saw the big sign on the wall which read,

"Just be Nice."

Everyone read the sign aloud and yelled out, "Yeah, yeah that's right. Just Be Nice. "

"Just Be Nice!   Yea!"

Sully was yelling too. He had decided not to be a bully any more. It was better to just be nice.

Ardzie started grinning and nodding his head.

He knew that he was going to have a great day at his new school with his new friends.

Everyone was going to

Just Be Nice

Vocabulary Builder

apologize   smirk   stutter
snout   bully   weird
tease   snicker   reluctant
              aardvark

Questions

1. What was the story about?

2. Who was your favorite character? Why?

3. Have you ever been bullied? If yes, what did you do?

4. Have YOU ever bullied anyone? If yes, did you feel badly? Why or why not?

5. What does "just be nice" mean to you?

Activities for Parents to Use

Here are a few practical activities that you can use to ensure that your child or love ones are actively helping to eliminate the problem of bullying. These activities must be ongoing to promote positive behavior in our homes and our communities.

1. Have colorful cards posted around the house (refrigerator, doors, bathroom mirror, etc) with the phrase "just be nice "

2. During mealtimes, discuss the importance of being nice.

3. Discuss what your child should do if someone mistreats him/her or say something unkind.

4. Make it a daily ritual to repeat the phrase "just be nice" several times during the day. Repetition can change behavior.

5. Do not allow any bullying in your household.

.6. Read and discuss this book with friends, family, acquaintances.

7.   Have a sleepover/or campout/or birthday celebration with your child's friends and read and discuss the book as one of your activities.

8.   Discuss with your child's teacher and other community organizations other activities that you can perform to help with the bullying problem.

9   Have your child wear the "Just Be Nice" wrist band. This is a conversation piece. Children and adults will ask about it when they see it. This further spreads the concept and perhaps will decrease bully behavior. (purchase thru our website www.sullythebully.com)

10.   Parents , take notice of any changed behavior with your child. (not wanting to go to school, headaches, not feeling well, despondent etc.)

 WORKING TOGETHER, WE CAN GET RID OF BULLYING! Let's start right now, today by simply spreading the words "Just be Nice"

About The Author
Miss Veronica

A graduate of Temple University with a BS degree in Education and graduate studies in Early Childhood Development, Miss Veronica has spent a number of years teaching and working with children. She has taught in the Philadelphia School System and has owned and operated a child care center in Wheaton, Maryland.

Her concern of the increase of bullying in our society and its negative effects on our youth led to her writing this book. It is Miss Veronica's view that bullying is behavior that should not be tolerated in our homes, our schools, or our communities. She envisions that if each of us continually practice the "Just be nice" concept, we will eventually see dramatic, positive effects in our fight against bullying.

11495722R00024

Made in the USA
Lexington, KY
13 October 2018